WHAT'S HAPPENING TO THE OZONE LAYER?

BY ISAAC ASIMOV

Gareth Stevens Publishing
MILWAUKEE

For a free color catalog describing Gareth Stevens' list of high-quality books, call 1-800-341-3569 (USA) or 1-800-461-9120 (Canada).

Library of Congress Cataloging-in-Publication Data

Asimov, Isaac, 1920-
   What's happening to the ozone layer? / by Isaac Asimov.
      p.   cm. -- (Ask Isaac Asimov)
   Includes bibliographical references and index.
   Summary: Describes the ozone layer and its ongoing destruction and explains what can be done to help solve the problem.
   ISBN 0-8368-0795-2
   1. Ozone layer--Juvenile literature. [1. Ozone layer.]
   I. Title. II. Series: Asimov, Isaac, 1920-   Ask Isaac Asimov.
   QC881.2.O9A75   1992
   551.5'112--dc20   92-5347

Edited, designed, and produced by
Gareth Stevens Publishing
1555 North RiverCenter Drive, Suite 201
Milwaukee, Wisconsin 53212, USA

Picture Credits
pp. 2-3, Paul Miller/Advertising Art Studios, 1992; pp. 4-5, © A. Leutscher/Natural Science Photos; pp. 6-7, Paul Miller/Advertising Art Studios, 1992; pp. 8-9, courtesy of NASA; pp. 10-11, Paul Miller/Advertising Art Studios, 1992; pp. 12-13, Paul Miller/Advertising Art Studios, 1992; pp. 14-15, Paul Miller/Advertising Art Studios, 1992; pp. 16-17, Paul Miller/Advertising Art Studios, 1992; pp. 18-19, Paul Miller/Advertising Art Studios, 1992; pp. 20-21, © Greenpeace/Greig; pp. 22-23, © Science VU/Visuals Unlimited; p. 24, © Science VU/Visuals Unlimited

Cover photograph, © Photo Library International/Robert Harding Picture Library: The gradual destruction of the ozone layer threatens this blue gem hanging in space, our Earth.

Series editor: Elizabeth Kaplan
Editor: Valerie Weber
Series designer: Sabine Beaupré
Picture researcher: Diane Laska

Printed in MEXICO

1 2 3 4 5 6 7 8 9 98 97 96 95 94 93 92

Contents

Words printed in **boldface** type the first time they occur in the text appear in the glossary.

Exploring Our Environment

Look around you. You see forests, fields, lakes, and rivers. You see farms, factories, houses, and cities. All of these things make up our **environment**. Things that you can't see are also part of the environment. For example, the environment includes the **atmosphere**, or the air all around us. The atmosphere has different layers. One layer is called the ozone layer. What is the ozone layer, and why is it important? Let's find out.

The Air Around Us

Several layers of gases surround the Earth, forming our atmosphere. Near the Earth, the atmosphere is the densest. It gets thinner and thinner the farther you go from our planet.

Different gases form layers at different distances from the Earth. Close to the Earth, **oxygen** and **nitrogen** are the main gases in the atmosphere. Between 12 and 30 miles (19-50 km) above the Earth's surface is a thin layer of gas called **ozone**. This layer helps protect us from some of the Sun's harmful rays.

7

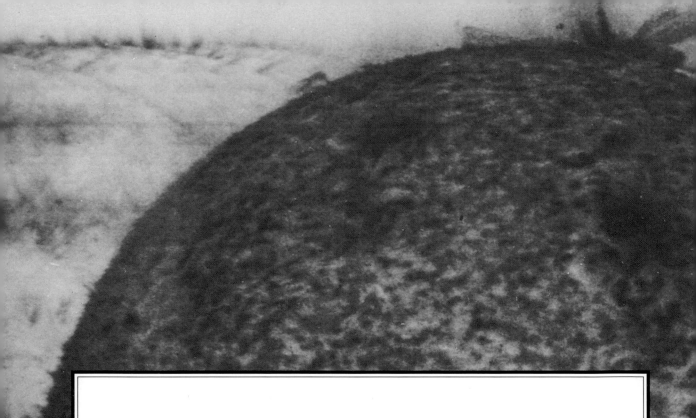

The Sun's Energy

The Sun gives off different kinds of energy. We feel some of the Sun's energy as heat. We see some of this energy as light. But the Sun also gives off energy we can't see or feel. Rays of **ultraviolet light** are one form of invisible energy from the Sun.

Although ultraviolet rays are invisible, they still affect us. These rays can burn our skin and cause problems with our eyes. People and other living things need protection from the Sun's ultraviolet rays.

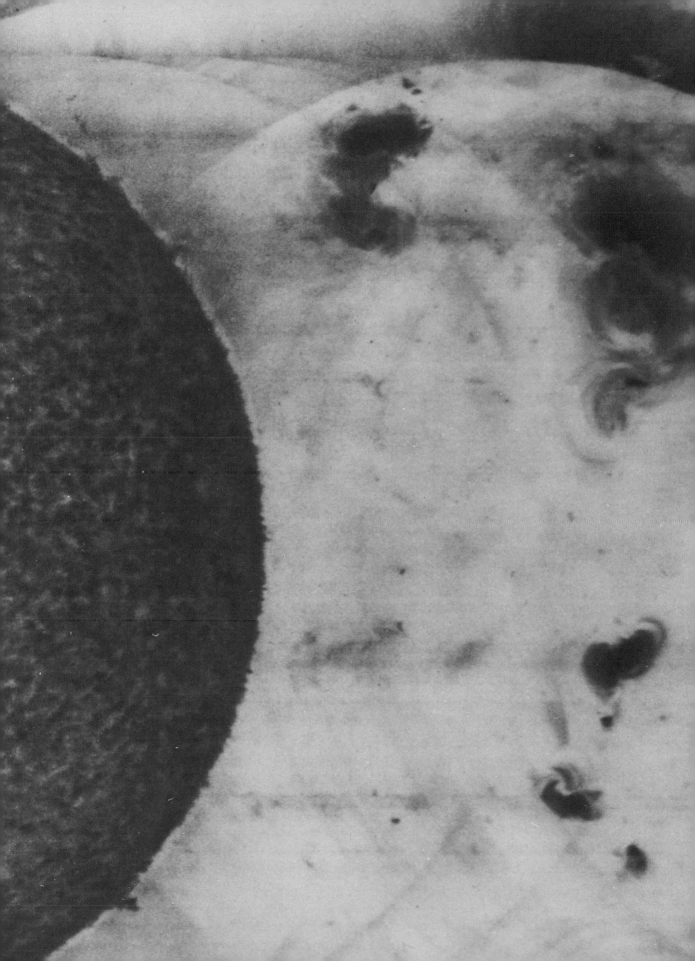

The Safety Shield

Ultraviolet light is so dangerous that life couldn't exist on Earth without a strong shield from these deadly rays. The ozone layer acts as our shield. The ozone in the upper atmosphere **absorbs** the energy of ultraviolet rays and turns it into heat. This stops most of the Sun's ultraviolet rays from reaching the surface of the Earth. With the ozone layer protecting us, we are shielded from most of the ultraviolet light that the Sun beams toward our planet.

A Hole in the Ozone

In recent years, we have learned that the ozone layer is thinning. Scientists have measured ozone in the upper atmosphere at different spots around the world. They have taken pictures of the ozone layer from Earth-orbiting satellites.

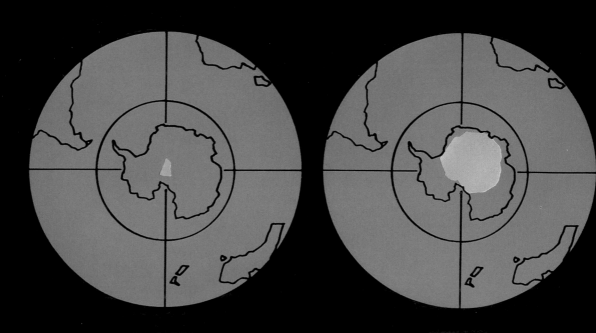

1979   1982

The measurements and pictures show that the ozone layer is being destroyed at a rapid rate. Each spring, a hole appears in the ozone layer over Antarctica. This hole is shown in pink. As you can see, each year that hole gets bigger and bigger.

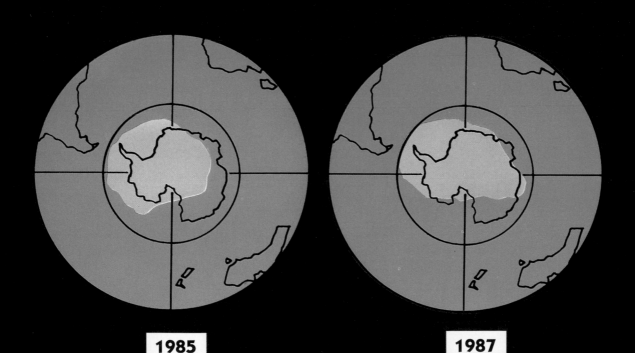

1985 **1987**

CFCs

Up, Up, and Away

Many scientists believe complex chemicals first made in the early 1900s are eating up the ozone layer. These chemicals are called **chlorofluorocarbons**, or CFCs for short. CFCs float in the air. They slowly move up to the ozone layer, where the Sun's ultraviolet rays break them down. The chemicals that result when CFCs break down react with the ozone in the upper atmosphere. In the past fifty years, these chemicals have steadily been destroying the ozone layer.

They're Everywhere

Chlorofluorocarbon gases are found in many household items. They are pumped through the coils on the back of refrigerators and in air conditioners. They fill the tiny plastic bubbles of plastic foam coolers and disposable plates and cups. The CFC gases make the containers light and suitable for serving hot or cold foods and drinks. But as these products have been destroyed over the past fifty years, billions of pounds of CFCs have been released into the air.

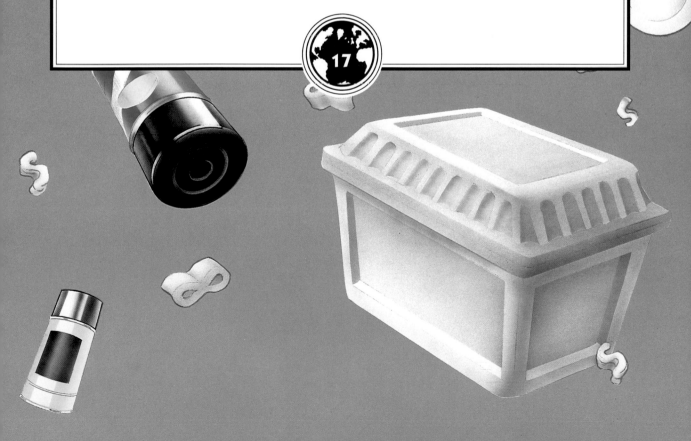

Trouble Brewing in the Air

The increased ultraviolet rays that come with the destruction of the ozone layer cause severe problems on Earth. People now have a greater chance of getting **skin cancer** from spending time outside in the Sun. **Photosynthesis**, the process by which plants make food, slows down. In the end, plants provide food for all other living things. So what's bad for plants is bad for all life on Earth. As more and more of the ozone layer is destroyed, all living things will suffer.

What Can You Do?

The best way to help stop the ozone layer
from being destroyed is to avoid using items
that contain CFCs. Ask your parents and
friends to avoid using disposable dishes
made out of plastic foam. If a restaurant
serves you food in these containers, ask them
to consider using other kinds of dishes instead.

You can also support groups working to ban
CFCs. They help persuade companies to find
safe substitutes for these dangerous chemicals.

A Long-term Problem

The destruction of the ozone layer is a long-term problem. Even if we stopped making CFCs today, these chemicals would keep leaking out of old appliances and plastic foam. But the ozone layer won't be safe until all traces of CFC gases disappear hundreds of years from now. Until then, we must let people know the dangers of CFCs and stop buying products that contain them. We <u>can</u> help the ozone layer and our planet recover.

More Books to Read

Air by Terry Jennings (Childrens Press)
Air Ecology by Jennifer Cochrane (Watts)
The Viking Children's World Atlas by J. Tivers and M. Day (Penguin)

Places to Write

Here are some places you can write to for more information about the ozone layer. Be sure to tell them exactly what you want to know about. Give them your full name and address so that they can write back to you.

National Center for
 Atmospheric Research
Information and Education
 Outreach Program
P.O. Box 3000
Boulder, Colorado 80307-3000

Environment Canada
 Inquiry Center
351 St. Joseph Boulevard
Hull, Quebec K1A 0H3

Friends of the Earth
218 D Street SE
Washington, D.C. 20003

Glossary

absorb (uhb-SORB): to take in; the ozone layer absorbs most ultra-violet light.

atmosphere (AT-muh-sfear): the gases that surround the Earth.

chlorofluorocarbon (klore-oh-floor-oh-KAHR-behn): chemicals found in refrigerators, air conditioners, and plastic foam containers; chlorofluorocarbons, also called CFCs, are destroying the ozone layer.

environment (en-VIE-run-ment): the natural and artificial things that make up the Earth.

nitrogen (NIE-troh-jehn): a colorless, odorless gas that makes up about four-fifths of the Earth's atmosphere.

oxygen (AHK-sih-jen): a colorless, odorless gas that makes up about one-fifth of the Earth's atmosphere.

ozone (OH-zohn): a gas related to oxygen; ozone forms a layer in the atmosphere that protects the Earth from the Sun's ultraviolet rays.

photosynthesis (pho-toh-SIN-theh-sis): the process by which green plants change carbon dioxide, which is a colorless gas, and water into food using the energy of the Sun.

skin cancer: a disease that occurs when the skin is damaged, often by overexposure to the Sun's ultraviolet rays.

ultraviolet (uhl-truh-VIE-uh-liht) **light**: invisible energy given off by the Sun that can damage the skin, the eyes, and other tissue of humans and animals.

Index